TABLE OF CONTENTS

DON'T START THE REVOLUTION WITHOUT ME: A REVIEW OF ARMY TRANSFORMATION

The world around us is changing. Political relationships, economic boundaries, technological limitations, and social interactions are continually redefined. War and the conduct of war as an expression of a nation's or peoples' political object is subject to similar turbulence. As these factors mix to shape the nature of future conflict, it is incumbent on military professionals to anticipate and predict the impact and plan accordingly to develop future security strategies, organizations, equipment, doctrine and roles. This process is not easy as it calls for an evaluation and balancing of present security risks against future. It further demands that one set aside existing preconceptions and presuppositions to evaluate current trends and developments and posit what they foretell for the future ones. The Army is undertaking this process in what is collectively termed transformation. Army transformation is defined as the "process that shapes the changing nature of military competition and cooperation through new combinations of concepts, capabilities, people and organizations."[1]

Service transformation is guided by specific directives detailed by the Department of Defense (DOD). By issuing planning guidance, DOD is attempting to define the context of the services transformation and tie their respective efforts to national security strategy and joint operational concepts.[2] In essence the goal is to shift from a threat-based to a capabilities-based paradigm. According to the direction, this process is enabled by the "historic opportunity" of the Cold War victory and current trends in technology development.[3] While laudatory in ambition, it remains to be seen whether this approach succeeds as a process for guiding change in military strategy and method. Some argue that by taking this path, we are having more impact in shaping adaptive asymmetric solutions for adversaries than in successfully anticipating and predicting future conflict.[4]

The nature and therefore conduct of war are constantly evolving. The construct of Clauswitz's description of war remains valid with the particular circumstances of physical and moral environments determining the nature of conflict.[5] The original theoretical model based on the rise of the modern nation-state as the dominant political apparatus and collective agreement between peoples is being challenged by the decline of the nation-state as the sole dominant polity. War continually changes, driven by the shifting plates of demographics, political forces, ethno-religious influences, economic factors, environmental influences, and technologic development. The change produces corresponding shifts within the relationship between the state, the population and the military. As these relationships shift, the means to achieve the political object of war also evolve. The evolution of military means and operations must also be constant and relevant to changes in the nature of war.

The importance of the discussion of future military capabilities takes on greater necessity because of these relatively recent changes in the nature of war. Throughout the collective American military experience and before, the nation-state has held a "monopoly of the use of violence."[6] The erosion of the state monopoly combined with the explosion in worldwide accessibility to weapons of mass destruction (WMD) places new emphasis on the need for an examination of how we view the nature of war and how we organize to operate. War remains a form of "community expression" used by a much broader number of actors than seen in the past.[7] The expansion in the number of actors begs the question of the continued relevance of existing methods and tools for the conduct of war. Changes in the structure, equipment and the techniques of military organizations must consider changes in the nature of war.

Periods of significant change in the nature of war and correspondingly the means to conduct war have been characterized as revolutions. Military revolutions have been defined as radical military innovations that fundamentally change the framework of war.[8] In their survey of western military innovation since 1300, Murray and Knox characterize five periods that have constituted fundamental change that have altered the social, political and military context of the times.[9] Each of these eras marked a fundamental shift in our understanding of war, the conduct of war, and the relationships between actors.. These periods begin with the creation of the existing international framework and carry us through the end of the Cold War and are characterized as follows:

- Establishment of the modern nation-state and national armed forces in the 17th century.

- Merger of national politics, population, and warfare of mass mobilization emerging in the French revolution.

- Amalgamation of the effects of the industrial revolution with mass mobilization in the mid to late 19th century.

- The first world war and the relationship between firepower and maneuver.

- The advent of nuclear weapons and the strategies of containment and deterrence.

Historian, Crane Brinton, through his study of the French Revolution determined that revolutions follow a distinct pattern that has been repeated in all modern revolutions to varying degrees.[10] While accepting cultural differences, he discovered that revolutions developed systematically following a set of rules almost like the growth and development of an organism. While used to examine distinct nation-state patterns of revolution, the sequential model of political and social revolutions serves as a useful tool in examining revolutions in military culture. Brinton used the metaphor of a fever for his "anatomy of revolution" equating the stages of a fever with those of a revolution:

- Prodromal/incubation stage – sets the context of the conditions that precede the outbreak of the actual revolution and defines the general factors that precipitated and contribute to the direction of the revolution.

- Symptomatic/moderate stage - the opening stages of a revolution that defines initial reactions to events.

- Crisis/radical stage – the apex or violent stage of the revolution where most significant change is initially instituted.

- Convalescence (recovery)/ moderate stage - the revolution moves back under the control of moderates and gains or changes are solidified and institutionalized.

Similarly, we will use this construct to assess the ongoing revolution in warfare, the Army response to date, and the outlook for future courses of action. To examine the current Army transformation discussion, it is essential to detail the origins of the debate. In this regard, this study explores four stages of the "revolution" chronologically as depicted below:

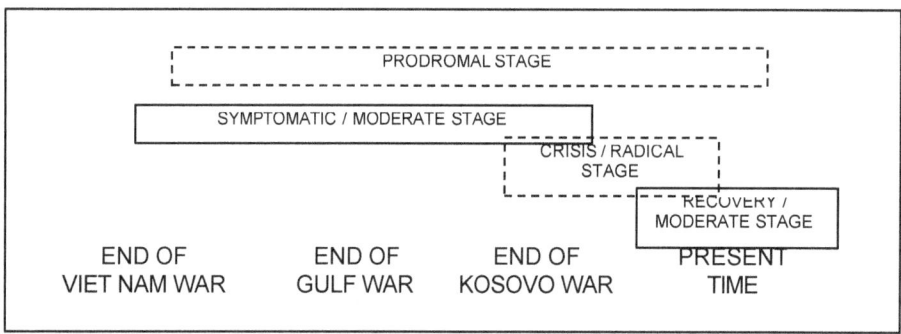

PRODROMAL/INCUBATION STAGE (DEFINING THE CONTEXT)

Each of us would be rich, if we had a nickel for every time we have heard "the world is different" since the end of the cold war. Of course, the reason for this comment is it is a fundamental truth. As depicted by journalist Robert D. Kaplan in his rather bleak view of an ever increasing anarchistic world: "we are entering a bifurcated world. Part of the globe is inhabited by Hegel's and Fukuyama's Last Man, healthy, well fed, and pampered by technology. The other, larger, part is inhabited by Hobbes's First Man, condemned to a life that is poor, nasty, brutish, and short. Although both parts will be threatened by environmental stress, the Last Man will be able to master it; the First Man will not."[11] Driven by a variety of forces including epidemic, crime, economic dislocation, ethno-cultural conflict, and competition for natural resources, the traditional global nation-state structure is under attack and has simply failed in some locations. All these factors contribute to the environment that is driving changes in the geo-political construct that dictates security strategy and the tools to implement that strategy.

The erosion of the nation-state hierarchy produces a reciprocal effect on future conflict and the means to resolve conflict. To this point, the focus of military thinkers has been largely in two areas: state-on-state conflict and internal security of the state. In the case of the United States, the former has been at the forefront of Army development since the end of the 19th century.[12] The focus of strategic thinking has shifted somewhat given the potential change in the types of conflict that the future holds. The decline in the global nation-state structure and the economic forces of globalization support the premise that we are moving to other forms of conflict.[13] Whatever the basis - ideological, cultural, or environmental conflict – the likelihood for the United States to conduct state-on-state war is declining while the dangers and likelihood of operating in areas of failed or failing states is increasing. The increased threat from weak or failed states has been recognized within the Department of Defense. The most recent Quadrennial Defense Review Report (QDR) identified "increasing challenges and threats emanating from territories of weak and failing states [where] the absence of capable or responsible governments creates a fertile ground for non-state actors engaging in drug trafficking, terrorism, and other activities that spread across borders."[14] The focal point centers on the outcomes and implications of this geo-strategic reordering and the resulting requirements or methodologies within a new security apparatus.

The operating environment within areas of failed or failing states is significantly different than when faced with a traditional nation-state based opponent or opponents. The operational and tactical battlefield is often described as asymmetric. These asymmetric relationships in military affairs and national security defined as "…acting, organizing, and thinking differently than opponents in order to maximize one's own advantages, exploit an opponent's weaknesses, attain the initiative, or gain greater freedom of action."[15] The dominance of U.S. conventional military power encourages others to pursue asymmetric means to counter our power. In essence, one does not play to an opposite's strength and instead attempts to turn their strengths into a military disadvantage. The debate on how best to deal with asymmetric threats has been a long standing discussion within the U.S. Army. It revolves around a problem of managing risk against perceived or real future threats and what is the principle role of the military. The Army's cultural bias which emerged in the latter half of the 19th century is to prepare for the next big war at the expense of a near term asymmetric dilemma.[16]

An additional ingredient in this evolving geo-political environment is the democratization of military power. The means to conduct individual or sustained acts of violence has spread throughout wide areas of Asia, Africa, and the Western Hemisphere to non-state actors as a result of the failure of state political structures and the effects of globalization.[17] Combining the potential of Weapons of Mass Destruction (WMD) capability, the economic resources from criminal activities such as narcotics trafficking, and an asymmetric operational outlook presents a particularly vexing problem to strategic planners. In particular, the fact that many non-state actors have an asymmetric values or interests to our own calls into question the utility of traditional strategies of deterrence that have served to counter more traditional political actors. In an environment devoid of tangible physical assets of value or a discernable organizational structure to target, the effectiveness of deterrence is debatable.[18] The anticipated global trends (continued regional dangers, the proliferation of advanced weapons and technologies, transnational dangers, and the increased danger of terrorist attacks) and asymmetric approaches combine to form "wild card" threats that could seriously challenge U.S. interests. It is deemed more likely that one or more wild cards threats will occur to challenge U.S. power than it is that none will occur in the near future.[19]

Changes in the global economic conditions contribute to an evolving strategic environment. Since the end of the Cold War, the differences in relative economic positions between regions and states around the world have come more into focus. Throughout undeveloped areas, the growth of poverty, economic inequality and the overwhelming indebtedness of governments which in turn place fewer and fewer resources into development, are all part of the broader trend in which resentment and hopelessness thrive.[20] Magnified by the influences of globalization, this resentment and unrealized expectations produce a recruiting pool for criminal and terrorist organizations. The outlook for improving these conditions does not appear good in the future with 50 nations classified as hyper-indebted.[21] These debtor states are incapable of meeting their obligations while simultaneously developing their domestic economies without some form of major financial assistance and restructuring. While globalization has produced some negative results, it has also served to increase the level of interaction and interdependence between national economies which further diminishes the likelihood of state-on-state conflict.[22] In this environment, the phenomenon of perpetually failed states (e.g. Haiti) becomes more the rule than the exception.

A second, but perhaps a more serious economic condition faces the United States and western European nations – balancing entitlement programs with revenues and the ability to sustain military power into the future. The Chairman of the Federal Reserve and the Congressional Budget Office (CBO) both project shortfalls in Medicare revenues relative to expenditures beginning in 2015 and a similar problem in Social Security budgeting in 2018. Given projected changes in demographics within the U.S. work force, federal spending would need to double as a percentage of Gross Domestic Product (GDP) to sustain current entitlement levels by 2035.[23] Western European nations face a similar, but more immediate problem. Based on their budget pressures it would appear unlikely that European nations will be able to increase levels of defense spending even in the short term. In the case of the United States, regardless of the manner that the entitlement question is ultimately resolved, the outlook for increased defense related spending in the future does not appear likely. Based on current defense plans, the CBO estimates for defense spending are a decline as a percentage of total federal budget through 2020 to a level where defense spending would be about 2% of GDP or the current level of many of our NATO allies.[24] While perhaps not directly impacting the debate on military transformation, the impact potentially drives the feasibility of pursuing various courses in military development. After all, funding is the engine of military power. It is as J. F. C. Fuller once commented on Grant that he "realized that as tactics are based on strategy, in its turn strategy is based on administration; that is, if action depends on movement, movement depends on supply."[25]

Technology continues to influence the elements of national power and shape the means of strategy. Technological change is being driven by forces in the private sector and adapted for military purposes to varying degrees around the world. The central technological phenomenon of our time is the development associated with the means and relative efficiency in processing information or more simply the Information Age. Perhaps the most profound impact of the current Information Age is the increased velocity of technological change and the sheer volume and distribution of technology throughout the world. Because of the rapid pace of technology and the accelerating nature of change, the ability and the usefulness of long range planning have been compressed. With the current pace of change, some have suggested that it is meaningless to try and project into the future. This view argues that the magnitude of change is beyond comprehension and human predictive abilities.[26] Given the pace of change and the often preeminent role of the private sector in shaping the development of technology, the potential exists for a state or non-state actor to quickly acquire military powers. Nations and non-state actors have demonstrated the ability to rapidly translate commercial technological power into its military equivalent.[27]

Furthermore, one cannot discount the impact of cultural bias towards technology and the application of technological solutions on American culture in general and American military culture in particular. One could characterize American culture as completely interwoven with the pursuit and benefits of technological applications. This complete integration of American culture and technology once caused President Calvin Coolidge to comment, "the man who builds a factory, builds a temple."[28] Our cultural proclivity has manifested itself to a degree that it produces a broadly-held belief in the redeeming powers of technology.[29] The danger associated with this dynamic is in seeking solutions to complex problems it could become the first or only option considered and implemented because it offers quick outcomes. It is a siren's call that leads us to hope that the complexities of thousands of years of political, cultural and social development of peoples can be understood and navigated through the sole correct application of a technological solution.

When considering revolutions, one thinks of a polity, society or organization in disequilibrium. Most of our thinking relative to changes of this nature has been associated with conditions that produce shifts in the equation of hard or military power. Over our recent experience, regional political instability precipitates a corresponding shift in security strategy to rebalance the equation. Clearly the scope and broad nature of multifaceted change is having a revolutionary impact on the global political and economic systems. This produces a reciprocal effect on military and security matters. The resulting environment produces a revolutionary impact on war and the conduct of war. The consequence of these results may not be categorized as one of revolutionary progress in warfare, but instead revolutionary devolution. This environment or disequilibrium has existed in terms of national security strategy since the end of the Cold War. The collapse of the Soviet Union precipitated the loss of the central vision of containment and deterrence that guided our actions for almost half a century. In fact, a popular current premise on transformation is that the world is changing too rapidly and unpredictably to accurately posit mid-to-long range threats. Indeed, the combination of a lack of a common direction and future vision while operating in the geo-political environment described in the paragraphs above creates unsolvable problems for the military planner. While these broad changes were profoundly impacting the environment, the Army had previously developed a methodology to guide the institution through uncertain times.

7

SYMPTOMATIC/MODERATE STAGE

The current Army transformation story had its roots in the end of the Viet Nam conflict. The Army emerged from Viet Nam committed to refocusing itself on the principle adversary faced – the Soviet Union. The single guiding focus of confronting Soviet bloc forces in central Europe served to galvanize all aspects of the Army and the broader defense community. In addressing its internal problems by the end of the Cold War, the Army is characterized as having rebuilt itself as an all-volunteer highly professional force which successfully integrated technologically sophisticated new equipment into a new operational doctrine.[30] Adding an exclamation point to the effectiveness of this process, in the minds of a generation of Army officers, this was the force that fought and won the first Gulf War and the process needed to guide future change within the Army.

The success of the Army model in the Gulf War is in large part responsible for the current debate in the direction of Army transformation. The lesson of the Gulf War, or more correctly, the lesson of the reemergence of the Army in the aftermath of the Viet Nam War is the importance of strategic ends in shaping ways and means. As stated previously, the strategic objective that the Army rediscovered after Viet Nam was its role in preparing to fight the Soviet Union. This common objective was the basis for Army reinvention efforts and served as the guiding focus for all Army modernization efforts in the intervening years.[31] This experience solidified the validity of the Army model for change in the institutional consciousness and has carried forward to the present as an effective means to balance innovation and risk.

The structure of the Army model for change was built on a common institutionally held view of the threat. From this model, flowed a well defined operational vision of future battlefields, a supporting doctrinal foundation, and associated tactics and procedures to successfully resolve battles and engagements. The model furthermore drove manpower, structure, equipment and training priorities to create a complete organization designed to meet its strategic requirements. For example, this construct led to the fielding of the "big five" systems of the M1 Abrams tank, M2 Bradley Fighting Vehicle, AH64 Apache helicopter, UH60 Blackhawk helicopter, and the Patriot missile system.[32] Furthermore, the Army model produced the Combat Maneuver Training Centers as part of this holistic approach. In reflecting back, the Army was justifiably proud of its accomplishments and felt well satisfied of the utility of a strategy-based approach toward future requirements.

Since the end of the Cold War and the first Gulf War, the Army and the broader defense community have not been idle in exploring the phenomena of the changing global environment. The Army sought to define the impact of global change would have on security matters and more specifically future requirements. The Army concluded that in a more complex world, devoid of a central threat, authoritative forecasts of the future could not be reached. However, Army leadership believed that the future environment could be characterized as an era of contradictory movements grouped around two "great forces" of geo-strategic change and the technical change incorporated into the Information Age.[33]

To best deal with this uncertain environment, the Army elected to retain a strategy-based approach to modernize the force and support the emerging two nearly-simultaneous Major Theater War (MTW) construct defined by the National Military Strategy (NMS). The two MTW approach was an innovation based on the proposition that the U.S. should prepare for the possibility that two regional conflicts could arise at the same time. If the U.S. were engaged in a conflict in one theater, an adversary in a second theater might try to gain his objectives with U.S. forces engaged elsewhere. This strategy was based on the assumption that the principle threat faced by the U.S. in the 1990's was a regional power and/or "rogue states."[34] The strategy identified "force packages" needed to achieve objectives. These force packages were based on an assessment of the combat capabilities and likely operations of potential adversaries, on the one hand, and the capabilities and doctrine of U.S. forces on the other. Recent operations in Desert Storm and potential operations in a Northeast Asia scenario served as the basic precept for this strategic construct and the frames of reference for tactical discussions by Army officers.

Simultaneously to dealing with this evolution in national strategy, the Army undertook two other ambitious restructuring initiatives. The first initiative was the draw down of forces on the heels of the Cold War victory. Albeit not self-initiated, the restructuring that occurred as a result of the draw down was a huge undertaking. In terms of active forces end strength the Army reduced from 765,000 to the end strength floor of 495,000 established by Congress in 1996.[35] Along with the reduction in manpower, the Army undertook a reciprocal draw down in associated force structure in both the active and reserve inventories and a divestiture of obsolete facilities particularly in Europe. Throughout the process, Army leadership sought to balance current force capability and readiness to support the "two MTW" strategy with the disruption produced by the effects of the drawdown. Besides the desire to achieve a peace dividend from the collapse of the Soviet Union, the Army sought to use end strength savings to pay for its force modernization initiatives.[36] However, the complete integration of strategy, modernization programs, and shared operational vision would only emerge at the end of the decade of the 1990s.

The Army initiated its first post Cold War change in doctrine and force design in 1993. Army Chief of Staff, General Gordon R. Sullivan recognizing the expansion of potential mission sets and the continuing rapid development of information technology "endorsed the concept of digitizing Army divisions, i.e., linking combat elements with sophisticated computers, enabling units to share situational awareness, and allowing commanders to make rapid, accurate tactical decisions."[37] This initiative, which grew into the FORCE XXI program the following year, was a result of a shared recognition by senior Army leaders on the need to develop a new force that could deal with future changes in the operational and tactical environment brought on by a variety of external forces. The methodology chosen was the creation of an experimentation force that would serve as the test bed for a variety of technological applications and a practical means to measure their utility for broader force-wide fielding.

In 1999 near the end of his tenure as Chief of Staff, General Dennis J. Reimer reported to Congress that the Army was a strategy-based force with a modernization program designed to support that strategy. With the backdrop of unprecedented levels of operational employment and tempo, Reimer stated that "the triumphs and failures of American military history can be traced through how well we have kept the demands of strategy and the requirements for military force in balance."[38] His testimony was a ringing endorsement of the post-Viet Nam modernization model used by the Army and a categorical statement of the requirement to link strategy to the evolution of force structure, equipment and doctrine. The implication was to do otherwise would risk rendering the military instrument ineffective and place soldier at risk.[39] The Reimer modernization program while closely tied to the NMS did not provide definitive statements on the nature of future battlefields. In the Army's collective mind, the regional threats of Iraq and North Korea replaced the Soviet Union as the bogey man to guide modernization efforts and doctrine.

The Army model for change was developed over a period of almost twenty years between the end of the Viet Nam conflict and the first Gulf War. It coalesced among a group of officers as the Army sought to reinvent itself after Viet Nam and was affirmed in the victory of the Gulf War. Central to the model was the linkage of modernization and force redesign to strategy or threat. Critical to successful implementation was a shared vision of the shape of future conflict by senior leaders and a commonly held recognition of the need to integrate new technology into the force.[40] It fell to the next Chief to provide a shift in transformational vision.

10

CRISIS/RADICAL STAGE

In the fall of 1999, the Army implemented the first complete version of the Army model for change seen since the end of the Gulf War. Unveiled by Army Chief of Staff, General Eric K. Shinseki, it marked a fundamental change to the threat-based approach used since the post-Viet Nam model. Tied to the NMS, the Army Transformation Vision called for the simultaneous change of the entire institution along three separate axes – Force, Institutional, and Concepts and Doctrine.[41] These axes would converge at a future point arriving as a completely transformed Army prepared to deal with the postulated future threats. The capabilities-based strategy for executing this transformation called for the development of an Interim Force equipped with Stryker Interim Armored Vehicle system to serve as a bridge to the future Objective Force equipped with the highly conceptual Future Combat System. To deal with current and near term requirements, the Army sought to maintain the Legacy Force or existing equipment and capabilities while fielding a new series of systems as part of the Interim force centered around the Stryker, the Crusader, and the Comanche. General Shinseki along with other senior leaders saw the opportunity for the Army to accept some short-term risk in order to accelerate change within the force during a window of opportunity in the strategic continuum.[42]

The Army Transformation plan marked a departure from the earlier threat-based modernization plans of the 1990's by attempting to complete the linkage between the theoretical models of future war to a broad array of changes across the Army. Perhaps influenced by recent events in Army support to the NATO-led mission in Kosovo, General Shinseki saw the need to fill a gap in Army capabilities exacerbated by changes in the strategic landscape.[43] The increase in asymmetric threats combined with an accelerating demand for the Army to perform non-traditional missions propelled the need to transform to a lighter more responsive force. In his view, the Army needed to become a lighter force less dependent on strategic transportation or face future irrelevance. Hence, the roadmap was a plan to guide the Army toward new capabilities and not a plan targeted toward a likely future threat.

To make the dramatic transition from a threats-based organization required assumptions about future conflict to guide research and development efforts. However, assumptions in terms of requirements for strategic mobility did not embody a common vision of future conflict shared throughout the Army. In addition, structural changes to the warfighting components of the Army were deferred for future debate within the Army. While the Transformation Campaign Plan articulated a future requirement, provided a roadmap to guide Army efforts and leveraged the Army's previous experience in managing change, it also sustained deployment of the next generation of Army combat systems and the traditional unit organization of employment and action.[44] While developed solely on the basis of broad guidance due to the lack of an overall DOD plan for military transformation, in the estimate of the Army, the Transformation Campaign Plan retained enough flexibility to adapt to evolving events.[45] The Army saw a process that would completely reinvent the institution in a matter of years versus decades and was well satisfied with the results. Without the common vision of future war, the capabilities-based model faced an uphill fight within the organization of the Army. Changes in political leadership added a further dimension to the debate.

The "Rumsfeld effect" real or imagined was felt almost immediately upon the Secretary's completion of his oath of office.[46] For the transformation community it marked in effect the fall of the Girondists and ultimately produced a complete change in the scope, tenor and direction of the Army. Secretary Rumsfeld assumed his duties with the promise of a fresh approach to DOD transformation and strategy from preceding administrations. The new Secretary's business background combined with his previous experience within the Department and his advocacy of missile defense initiatives led many beltway pundits to conclude that a new harmonious period of civil-military relations were in the offing. Secretary Rumsfeld quickly proved that he was prepared to chart a path little used since the "New Look" era during the Eisenhower administration to shape military strategy and transformation.[47]

Beginning in February 2001, Secretary Rumsfeld directed a series of contentious reviews of existing plans, programs and policies. This review culminated with the publication of the Quadrennial Defense Review Report (QDR) in September 2001. The QDR provided more specific Departmental guidance than the services had seen in years. Addressing six specific areas to guide all DOD transformation efforts, the Secretary was attempting to coordinate what had previously become increasingly disparate service transformation initiatives.[48] While quite content with the Transformation Campaign Plan it had developed in 1999, the Army would reap the lion share of DOD backlash for attempting to define its own strategic vision. The new Chief of the Office of Force Transformation, retired Vice Adm. Arthur Cebrowski, had a decidedly different approach focused on an emerging theory of war that derived power from information, access and speed. He believed that it was not sufficient to say we fight and win the nation's wars, instead the mission becomes dissuading military competition.[49] The QDR process articulated a shift in security strategy and the fundamental process of military innovation and change. Within DOD, the events of September 11, 2001, and its aftermath would shape process and the vision of future conflict.

"Instead of building our armed forces around plans to fight this or that country, we need to examine our vulnerabilities...and then fashion our forces as necessary to deter and defeat that threat," wrote Secretary Rumsfeld in arguing for a focus on the growing asymmetric threat confronting the United States and a shift to a capabilities-based approach to transformation.[50] In shaping DOD direction for transformation, the approach the Secretary adopted heeded the citation of Winston Churchill that the era of procrastination, half-measures, and baffling expedients was at an end.[51] The Army Transformation Campaign Plan with its sequential linear approach in moving from the current force to the future seemed an obvious candidate for close scrutiny. Two flaws quickly emerged in comparing the Army plan with the new DOD transformational goals. First, eighteen systems in the Army procurement pipeline were deemed not in line with new defense strategy, and second, the failure on the Army's behalf to identify plans to address future warfighting organizational innovations. These flaws fueled a general perception that the Army was resistant to substantive transformation. Because of this perception, DOD would take a heavy hand in redirecting Army transformation efforts and culminating with the departure of the Army Secretary and General Shinseki from their respective posts in April and June 2003.[52]

CONVALESCENCE/MODERATE STAGE?

Since the summer of 2003, the direction of Army transformation has shifted dramatically. Demands of current mission requirements have played a role in redefining priorities, however, the engagement of DOD in the transformation process, in large part because of the interest of Secretary Rumsfeld, owns the lion share of responsibility for this shift. In his 2003 Report to Congress, the Secretary states, "over the past year, the military departments have each proposed their individual models of how they would prefer to fight…we are now seeking to integrate these perspectives into an overarching concept for the employment of the joint force."[53] The report goes on to highlight the termination of 24 Army systems combined with a reduction of 24 others, in order to invest in the Future Combat System. Before the end of 2003, the Army had completely reviewed and reengineered the transformation azimuth. The Army Transformation strategy dropped the multiple axes approach built focused on system acquisition and instead focuses on three components: Army culture, process transformation, and the development of inherently joint capabilities.[54] The revised strategy is closely linked with the recently developed joint operational concepts and the DOD planning guidance issued earlier in the year. In fact, the three components of Army transformation mirror the overarching DOD guidance virtually verbatim.[55] It is clear the corporate Army got the message.

The prognosis of the future success of Army transformation efforts is difficult to predict. Certainly, the long term outlook for funding to sustain the acquisition of future systems is not promising if one heeds the warnings of the Federal Reserve Chairman. However, assuming that funding will be available to procure future technologies, it is not clear how the transition from the current to future force increases effectiveness in future conflict with expanding asymmetric threats. The ongoing transition and experimentation to increase modularity of the combat formations is a promising first step. Ultimately, achieving the required characteristics of the future force requires a much broader examination of the Army.

The examination should approach the problem of the future Army in much the same way as our predecessors at the end of Viet Nam by defining requirements based on a shared vision of future battlefields. Critical in the formulation of this shared vision is an informed debate on future conflict. However, requirements should focus on types of structures, formations and soldiers needed for success. For example, the construct of an Army built around eighteen year old high school graduates trained in a relatively short period may not produce successful results in the future. The increasing complexity and decentralization in operations may require soldiers with higher degree of intellectual maturity than the current standard recruit who has demonstrated only a basic level of physical and mental acumen. If indeed the quality of soldier needs to change, it is likely that formations must also be changed. Certainly, the costs associated with attracting a better educated more mature recruit would not allow us to maintain current force levels or existing structure.

The need to further reform organizational structure has other compelling reasons besides cost. Effectiveness in operations is diminished due to the maintenance of pyramidal organizational arrangements that are little changed since our grandfathers' service. While noting the inherent differences between combat and support missions, retaining multiple layers of command is inherently inefficient as each layer adds friction to the flow of information and control. The decentralized nature of future operations points toward a serious examination of these arrangements as we continue the transition from the current to future force. Restructuring our forces and recreating our processes is absolutely essential to maintain our qualitative advantage over potential competitors.

The current level of defense spending that we enjoy is not a guarantee of the future. Competing demands for federal funding will likely reduce future defense spending. In addition, the rate of technological change has accelerated and our relative advantage could diminish comparatively and in a very short time. Combining the unprecedented pace of technological change with the increase of asymmetric threats means we cannot afford to be satisfied with our current forces or their immediate derivatives. The basic objectives of DOD and Army transformation efforts are to evolve department culture, reinvent processes and enhance joint

14

force capabilities. Using the current force as a baseline, the strategy directs an assessment and comparison of new operating concepts that utilize new organizational constructs, capabilities and doctrines. Investment decisions will be made from this process.

The Army's model for change that emerged in the late 1970's achieved incremental enhancement to capabilities over several decades. Beginning in 1999, the Army initiated a transformational effort to reinvent itself and correct identified shortfalls in capability. This approach accepted risk to the current force in order to fund development of future combat systems envisioned to equip the objective force. In the fall of 2003, the Army scrapped the multiple axis's approach and "rebalanced the equation" relative to funding the current force. Citing ongoing operational needs, a reevaluation of funding levels has reversed the paradigm of the past four years and shifted priority to current requirements from future system developments. The central reason for this change in Army approach was the engagement of DOD and Secretary Rumsfeld into an area that had been left as a service purview for decades. If left to its own devices, the Army would have followed an established approach which while limiting risk would have fallen short in producing the type of force needed in the future. The threat-based model would have likely focused on traditional conventional threats unless compelled by events. The current capabilities-based strategy remains a work in progress with tremendous potential, but with a wide array of institutional forces remaining in its path.

WORD COUNT=6,353

ENDNOTES

[1] Department of the Army, *Army Transformation Roadmap*, (Washington, D.C.: U.S. Department of the Army, 1 November 2003), ix.

[2] Department of Defense, *Transformation Planning Guidance*, (Washington, D.C.: U.S. Department of Defense, April 2003), 3.

[3] Ibid, 5.

[4] Eliot A. Cohen and John Gooch, *Military Misfortunes: The Anatomy of Failure in War*, (New York, Anchor Books, 1990), 237-238.

[5] Raymond Aron, *Clausewitz: Philosopher of War*, (New York, Simon and Schuster, 1976), 119.

[6] Michael Howard, *The Causes of War*, (Cambridge, Harvard University Press, 1983), 34-35.

[7] James M. Dubik, "Has Warfare Changed? Sorting Apples from Oranges, " *Landpower Essay* 02-3 (July 2002), 4.

[8] MacGregor Knox and Williamson Murray, *The Dynamics of Military Revolution: 1300-2050*, (Cambridge, Cambridge University Press, 2001), 6.

[9] Ibid

[10] Crane Brinton, *The Anatomy of Revolution*, (New York, Random House, 1965), 250.

[11] Robert D. Kaplan, "The Coming Anarchy," *The Atlantic Monthly* 273 no 2 (February 1994): 44-76.

[12] Brian McAllister Linn, "Peacetime Transformation in the U.S. Army," in Transforming Defense, ed Conrad C. Crane (Carlisle Barracks, Strategic Studies Institute, 2001), 8.

[13] Douglas A. MacGregor, Transformation Under Fire: Revolutionizing How America Fights, (Westport, Praeger Press, 2003), 40-41.

[14] Department of Defense, *Quadrennial Defense Review Report*, (Washington, D.C.: U.S. Department of Defense, 30 September 2001), 5.

[15] Steven Metz and Douglas V. Johnson II, *Asymmetry and US Military Strategy: Definition, Background, and Strategic Concepts*, (Carlisle, Strategic Studies Institute, 2001), 5.

[16] Arthur P. Wade,"The Military Command Structure: The Great Plains, 1853-1891," *Journal of the West 15* (July 1978): 18-19.

[17] QDR, 5.

[18] Colin S. Gray, *Maintaining Effective Deterrence*, (Carlisle, Strategic Studies Institute, 2003), 23.

[19] Department of Defense, *Quadrennial Defense Review Report*, (Washington, D.C.: U.S. Department of Defense, May 1997), section 2.

[20] Saskia Sassen, Governance Hotspots: Challenges We Must Confront in the Post-September 11th World, (Chicago, University of Chicago, 2002), 4.

[21] Ibid, 6.

[22] Allan Greenspan, "Globalization, Remarks at the Banco de Mexico Anniversary Conference," The International Experience (November 2000), 14.

[23] Nathan Littlefield, "The $45 Trillion Problem," *The Atlantic Monthly* 293 no 1 (January 2004): 146.

[24] Congressional Budget Office, *The Long-term Implications of Current Defense Plans* (Washington, D.C.: U.S. Congressional Budget Office, January 2003), i-iii.

[25] J.F.C. Fuller, *The Generalship of Ulysses S. Grant,* (Bloomington, Indiana University Press, 1970, 214.

[26] Judith Berman, "Science Fiction without a Future," The New York Review of Science Fiction 13 no 9 (May 2001): 6.

[27] Gray, 23.

[28] Calvin Coolidge, *Have Faith in Massachusetts*, (Boston, Houghton Mifflin, 1919), 14.

[29] Klaus Benesch,"Technology and American Culture," *American Studies* 41 no 3 (Autumn 1996): 331.

[30] Department of the Army, *The Army of Desert Storm* , (Washington, D.C., Center for Military History, November 2001) 26.

[31] Barry R. McCaffrey, "Lessons of Desert Storm," *Joint Forces Quarterly* (Winter 2000): 13

[32] Department of the Army, *Force XXI Operations*, (Ft. Monroe, TRADOC Pam 525-2, November 1999), para. 1-1a.

[33] Steven Metz, *Revising the Two MTW Force Shaping Paradigm* , (Carlisle Barracks, Strategic Studies Institute, 2001), 2.

[34] Ibid

[35] General Accounting Office, *Force Structure: Army Support Forces Can Meet Two-Conflict Strategy with Some Risks* (Washington, D.C., U.S. General Accounting Office, February 1997), 2.

[36] Ibid

[37] Combat Studies Institute, *Sixty years of Reorganizing for Combat: A Historical Trend Analysis*, (Ft. Leavenworth, CSI Press, January 2000), 50-51.

[38] Congress, Senate, Committee on Armed Forces, Subcommittee on Airland Forces, Statement on Modernization by General Dennis J. Reimer, 106th Cong., 1st sess., 24 March 1999, 1.

[39] Ibid

[40] General Accounting Office, *Military Transformation: Army Has a Comprehensive Plan for Managing Its Transformation but Faces Major Challenges* (Washington, D.C., U.S. General Accounting Office, November 2001), 2.

[41] Department of the Army, *Army Transformation Roadmap*, (Washington, D.C.: U.S. Department of the Army, November 2002) 42.

[42] Larry R. Ellis, "The Transformation Campaign Plan: The Tool to Transform the Army," *Army Magazine* 50 no. 10 (October 1999): 26.

[43] CSI Reports, 62.

[44] Department of the Army, *Objective Force 2015*, (Washington, D.C.: U.S. Department of the Army, December 2002) 7-8.

[45] "How Transformational is Army Transformation?," *AUSA National Security Report* (February 2003): 9.

[46] Robert Kagan, "Calculating the Rumsfeld Effect," *Washington Post*, 19 January 2001. [journal on line] available from http://www.newamericancentury.org/defense-20010119.htm . Internet. Accessed 15 February 2004.

[47] Herman S. Wolk, "The New Look," *Air Force Magazine*, vol 86 no. 8, August 2003. [journal on line] available from http://www.afa.org/magazine/aug2003/0803look.html Internet. Accessed 23 February 2004.

[48] QDR, 5.

[49] Arthur K. Cebrowski, "An Interview with the Director," ITAA August 2002, 1-3.

[50] Donald H. Rumsfeld, "Transforming the Military," *Foreign Affairs* 81 no 3 (May/June 2002): 20.

[51] George W. Bush, "Speech at Citadel," White House Transcript, 23 September 1999. [journal on line] available from http://usinfo.state.gov/topical/pol/terror/01121002.htm Accessed 18 January 2004.

[52] Vernon Loeb, "Rumsfeld Turns Eye to Future of Army," Washington Post, 8 June 2003, p. A12.

[53] Donald H. Rumsfeld, 2003 Annual Report to Congress, (Washington, D.C.: U.S. Department of Defense, September 2003), 8.

[54] Army Transformation Roadmap 2003, ix.

[55] Transformation Planning Guidance, 8-9.

BIBLIOGRAPHY

Army Transformation Roadmap, Department of the Army, (Washington, D.C.: U.S. Department of the Army, November 2002).

Army Transformation Roadmap, Department of the Army, (Washington, D.C.: U.S. Department of the Army, 1 November 2003).

Aron, Raymond, *Clausewitz: Philosopher of War*, (New York, Simon and Schuster, 1976).

Berman, Judith, "Science Fiction without a Future," The New York Review of Science Fiction 13 no 9 (May 2001).

Benesch, Klaus, "Technology and American Culture," *American Studies* 41 no 3 (Autumn 1996).

Brinton, Crane, *The Anatomy of Revolution*, (New York, Random House, 1965).

Bush, George W., "Speech at Citadel," White House Transcript, 23 September 1999. [journal on line] available from http://usinfo.state.gov/topical/pol/terror/01121002.htm Accessed 18 January 2004.

Cebrowski, Arthur K., "An Interview with the Director," ITAA August 2002.

Cohen, Eliot A. and John Gooch, *Military Misfortunes: The Anatomy of Failure in War*, (New York, Anchor Books, 1990).

Coolidge, Calvin, *Have Faith in Massachusetts*, (Boston, Houghton Mifflin, 1919).

Dubik, James M., "Has Warfare Changed? Sorting Apples from Oranges, " *Landpower Essay* 02-3 (July 2002).

Ellis, Larry R., "The Transformation Campaign Plan: The Tool to Transform the Army," *Army Magazine* 50 no. 10 (October 1999).

Force Structure: Army Support Forces Can Meet Two-Conflict Strategy with Some Risks, General Accounting Office, (Washington, D.C., U.S. General Accounting Office, February 1997).

Force XXI Operations, Department of the Army, (Ft. Monroe, TRADOC Pam 525-2, November 1999).

Fuller, J.F.C., *The Generalship of Ulysses S. Grant,* (Bloomington, Indiana University Press, 1970.

Gray, Colin S., *Maintaining Effective Deterrence*, (Carlisle, Strategic Studies Institute, 2003).

Greenspan, Allan, "Globalization, Remarks at the Banco de Mexico Anniversary Conference," The International Experience (November 2000).

How Transformational is Army Transformation?, *AUSA National Security Report* (February 2003).

Howard, Michael, *The Causes of War*, (Cambridge, Harvard University Press, 1983).

Kagan, Robert, "Calculating the Rumsfeld Effect," *Washington Post*, 19 January 2001. [journal on line] available from http://www.newamericancentury.org/defense-20010119.htm . Internet. Accessed 15 February 2004.

Kaplan, Robert D., "The Coming Anarchy," *The Atlantic Monthly* 273 no 2 (February 1994).

Knox, MacGregor and Williamson Murray, *The Dynamics of Military Revolution: 1300-2050*, (Cambridge, Cambridge University Press, 2001).

Linn, Brian McAllister, "Peacetime Transformation in the U.S. Army," in Transforming Defense, ed. Conrad C. Crane (Carlisle Barracks, Strategic Studies Institute, 2001).

Littlefield, Nathan, "The $45 Trillion Problem," *The Atlantic Monthly* 293 no 1 (January 2004).

Loeb, Vernon, "Rumsfeld Turns Eye to Future of Army," Washington Post, 8 June 2003.

MacGregor, Douglas A., Transformation Under Fire: Revolutionizing How America Fights, (Westport, Praeger Press, 2003).

McCaffrey, Barry R., "Lessons of Desert Storm," *Joint Forces Quarterly* (Winter 2000).

Metz, Steven, *Revising the Two MTW Force Shaping Paradigm* , (Carlisle Barracks, Strategic Studies Institute, 2001).

Metz, Steven and Douglas V. Johnson II, *Asymmetry and US Military Strategy: Definition, Background, and Strategic Concepts*, (Carlisle, Strategic Studies Institute, 2001).

Military Transformation: Army Has a Comprehensive Plan for Managing Its Transformation but Faces Major Challenges, General Accounting Office, (Washington, D.C., U.S. General Accounting Office, November 2001).

Objective Force 2015, Department of the Army, (Washington, D.C.: U.S. Department of the Army, December 2002).

Quadrennial Defense Review Report, Department of Defense, (Washington, D.C.: U.S. Department of Defense, May 1997).

Quadrennial Defense Review Report, Department of Defense, (Washington, D.C.: U.S. Department of Defense, 30 September 2001).

Rumsfeld, Donald H., "Transforming the Military," *Foreign Affairs* 81 no 3 (May/June 2002).

Rumsfeld, Donald H., 2003 Annual Report to Congress, (Washington, D.C.: U.S. Department of Defense, September 2003).

Sassen, Saskia, Governance Hotspots: Challenges We Must Confront in the Post-September 11th World, (Chicago, University of Chicago, 2002).

Sixty years of Reorganizing for Combat: A Historical Trend Analysis, Combat Studies Institute, (Ft. Leavenworth, CSI Press, January 2000).

Statement on Modernization by General Dennis J. Reimer, Congress, Senate, Committee on Armed Forces, Subcommittee on Airland Forces, , 106th Cong., 1st sess., 24 March 1999.

The Army of Desert Storm, Department of the Army, (Washington, D.C., Center for Military History, November 2001).

The Long-term Implications of Current Defense Plans, Congressional Budget Office, (Washington, D.C.: U.S. Congressional Budget Office, January 2003).

Transformation Planning Guidance, Department of Defense, (Washington, D.C.: U.S. Department of Defense, April 2003).

Wade, Arthur P., "The Military Command Structure: The Great Plains, 1853-1891," *Journal of the West 15* (July 1978).

Wolk, Herman S., "The New Look," *Air Force Magazine*, vol 86 no. 8, August 2003. [journal on line] available from http://www.afa.org/magazine/aug2003/0803look.html Internet. Accessed 23 February 2004.

www.ingramcontent.com/pod-product-compliance
Lightning Source LLC
Chambersburg PA
CBHW081813280526
45789CB00008B/3121